Lerner SPORTS™

SPORTS VIPs

MEET JULIO RODRÍGUEZ

LESLIE HOLLERAN

Lerner Publications ◆ Minneapolis

Lerner Publications Company
An imprint of Lerner Publishing Group, Inc.
241 First Avenue North
Minneapolis, MN 55401 USA

For reading levels and more information, look up this title at www.lernerbooks.com.

Main body text set in Aptifer Slab LT Pro. Typeface provided by Linotype AG.

Editor: Anne E. Hill

Library of Congress Cataloging-in-Publication Data

Names: Holleran, Leslie, author.
Title: Meet Julio Rodríguez : Seattle Mariners superstar / Leslie Holleran.
Description: Minneapolis : Lerner Publications, [2025] | Series: Lerner sports. Sports VIPs | Includes bibliographical references and index. | Audience: Ages 7–11 years | Audience: Grades 4–6 | Summary: "Seattle Mariners center fielder Julio Rodríguez can hit home runs, steal bases, and make diving catches in the outfield. He's one of MLB's best, and youngest, superstars. Explore his life and career"— Provided by publisher.
Identifiers: LCCN 2024023801 (print) | LCCN 2024023802 (ebook) | ISBN 9798765649268 (lib. bdg.) | ISBN 9798765662465 (pbk.) | ISBN 9798765658550 (epub)
Subjects: LCSH: Rodríguez, Julio, 2000-—Juvenile literature. | Center fielders (Baseball)—United States—Biography—Juvenile literature. | Baseball players—Dominican Republic—Biography—Juvenile literature. | Seattle Mariners (Baseball team)—Juvenile literature. | Baseball—Washington (State)—Seattle—History—Juvenile literature. | Olympic athletes—Dominican Republic—Biography—Juvenile literature.
Classification: LCC GV865.R623 H65 2025 (print) | LCC GV865.R623 (ebook) | DDC 769.357092 [B]—dc23/eng/20240703

LC record available at https://lccn.loc.gov/2024023801
LC ebook record available at https://lccn.loc.gov/2024023802

Manufactured in the United States of America
1-1011066-53538-8/23/2024

TABLE OF CONTENTS

HISTORIC HOT STREAK

Julio Rodríguez was sizzling with the bat in August 2023. He had already broken a Major League Baseball (MLB) record. He also had the best batting average in the American League (AL).

The high point of Rodríguez's hot streak came on August 19. He banged his 17th hit in four games. The record number of hits in four straight MLB games had been 16. Rodríguez didn't know he was making history. Then he saw it on the scoreboard.

FAST FACTS

DATE OF BIRTH: December 29, 2000
POSITION: center field
LEAGUE: MLB

PROFESSIONAL HIGHLIGHTS: named the 2022 AL Rookie of the Year; named an All-Star in 2022 and 2023; played with the bronze medal–winning Dominican Republic Olympic team in 2021

PERSONAL HIGHLIGHTS: grew up in the Dominican Republic; donates his time and money helping young people in his hometown; has the nickname J-Rod

Julio Rodríguez at bat against the Houston Astros in August 2023

Even Seattle Mariners manager Scott Servais was in awe. "I've never seen anything like it. Nobody in the [recent] history of MLB has seen anything like it," he said. "But what can you say? Julio is just smoking hot right now."

Rodríguez's record streak pushed the Mariners back into the AL playoff race. The league named him August's Player of the Month. He was the first Mariners player in eight years to get the honor. MLB's latest superstar was just getting started. It was only his second season in the majors.

Rodríguez rounds second base.

CHAPTER 1

Julio's father wanted to play professional baseball, but he never made it to MLB. Instead, he passed on his dream to his son. Once Julio could walk, his dad began tossing him balls in the backyard. He gave Julio his first glove.

As Julio got older, he played baseball with his schoolmates. At 10, he was playing in a local league with older kids. His teammates were three to four years older. At 12, he hit his first home run.

Rodríguez, then 18, in a minor-league game in July 2019

SUPER SPORTS SCOOP

Many great Dominican MLB players inspired Julio to play baseball. They include Nelson Cruz, David Ortiz, and Alex Rodriguez, whose nickname is A-Rod. Julio's nickname is J-Rod.

Julio's dad trained him until he was 14. His father left work an hour early to practice with his son. "I missed time at work. For me that was very difficult," Julio's father said.

The missed time was worth the effort. Julio excelled at baseball. His parents encouraged their son's dreams. But they also expected him to finish high school. They wanted him to have an education in case his MLB dreams didn't work out.

CHAPTER 2

YOUNG STANDOUT

At 13, Julio went to a Dominican Prospect League event. Amateur players got the chance to show off their skills there. Julio was noticed by trainer Juan Francisco Peña from MB Baseball Academy.

Santiago de los Caballeros, Dominican Republic

Peña invited Julio to visit the academy in the Dominican city of Santiago de los Caballeros. Julio's dad agreed to drive him to the city three hours away. This was an important opportunity. Sports agents would be there. Agents represent athletes in business deals, such as signing contracts with teams.

During the visit, Julio stood out among hundreds of other players. He could hit the ball much farther than the others. People wondered who he was and where he came from. He got the attention of agent Ulises Cabrera.

Soon, Peña, Cabrera, and the Rodríguez family made an agreement. Julio would train with Peña at the academy. He would finish high school from there.

Rodríguez celebrates with his Seattle Mariners teammates in a game against the Toronto Blue Jays in July 2024.

Julio's dad had been training him to be a catcher. That had been his dad's position. But at the academy, Julio trained to be an outfielder. Julio also began learning English. He went to school on Saturdays for lessons. His parents insisted he finish high school and learn English. They knew it would help him in MLB.

In 2017, Julio signed a contract with the Seattle Mariners for $1.75 million. He was just 16. The team believed in his skills. But he was not going to play in MLB right away.

SUPER SPORTS SCOOP

Julio was named the Dominican Summer League (DSL) Most Valuable Player in 2018. He led the league in almost every hitting category. He was also named an All-Star.

Rodríguez at the Seattle Mariners Photo Day in February 2020

Julio made his professional debut on the Mariners DSL minor-league team in 2018. The DSL is the only rookie league in Latin America. He was three years younger than the average player in the league.

The next fall, Julio went to the Mariners high-performance camp. He spent more than two months gaining skills to support his game. He learned to exercise to make his body stronger, eat healthful food, and become mentally prepared for games.

Rodríguez swings the bat during a game for the minor-league team West Virginia Power.

CHAPTER 3

OLYMPIC MEDALIST

Rodríguez played in the minors again in 2019. He was anxious to move up. His season began in West Virginia. He then played on Seattle's Class A-Advanced team in California. By October, he was ranked as the Mariners number two prospect. He was 25th on MLB's Top 100 Prospects list.

Rodríguez watched other players move on to MLB. He couldn't wait for his chance. But he needed to put in more time to prove he belonged there. Then he was hit in the hand with a pitch. His season was cut short by a broken bone. He played in only 84 games in the summer of 2019. He had hoped to play many more.

Rodríguez makes a leaping catch in right field during a minor-league game in September 2019.

Rodríguez is ready to swing the bat during a minor-league game.

Rodríguez was more than just a top prospect. He was also a team player. He wanted his teammates to succeed as much as he did. This was clear to Mariners general manager Jerry Dipoto. He said, "Julio is a loving teammate. He cares about everybody. He cares about the game. He loves what he's doing."

Rodríguez's hand healed. His play got even better. He also played for his country as he worked his way up to the majors. He spent a month playing with the Dominican team at the 2020 Olympic Games in Tokyo, Japan (held in 2021 due to the COVID-19 pandemic). The Dominican team defeated South Korea 10–6. Rodríguez and his teammates won the bronze medal.

Winning an Olympic medal was exciting. "We did it. I still can't believe we made history and my name will be

SUPER SPORTS SCOOP

When Rodríguez played with the Dominican Olympic baseball team, he was the team's youngest player. The Dominican Republic's bronze medal was its first-ever medal in baseball.

Rodríguez hits a two-run home run playing for the Dominican Republic at the 2020 Summer Olympic Games in Tokyo.

attached to an Olympic medal forever. That stage was so big that I never thought I would be on it," Rodríguez said.

Late in 2021, Rodríguez got closer to making his major league debut. The Mariners added him to their 40-man roster. This meant he could be called up to the majors at any time. He was about to get his big-league chance.

CHAPTER 4

TAKING SEATTLE BY STORM

Rodríguez's major league career got off to a rough start in 2022. Some said he was subjected to rookie treatment by umpires. They seemed to be harder on him than on the players with more experience. The umpires called him out on strikes 30 times in 20 games that April.

Rodríguez didn't let it get him down. Servais said, "I give all the credit in the world to Julio. Not many people can handle things the way he has. . . . He has not changed his approach [to batting]." Pitchers soon realized he would rarely try to hit pitches outside the strike zone. They began to throw him more pitches he could handle, and his luck at the plate changed.

Rodríguez runs around the bases after hitting a two-run home run against the San Diego Padres in July 2022.

In July 2022, he was invited to the MLB All-Star Game. From there, Rodríguez's debut season just kept getting better. He helped the Mariners advance to their first playoffs in 21 years. In August, he signed a new contract with the Mariners. The deal would pay him at least $210 million over the next 12 years.

After his great rookie season, Rodríguez chose to give back. He donated to his hometown. He gave Loma

SUPER SPORTS SCOOP

Rodríguez hit 81 home runs at MLB's Home Run Derby in July 2022. The derby is an annual contest held the day before the All-Star Game. He came in second in the derby behind New York Yankees outfielder Juan Soto.

de Cabrera a new ambulance. The city had not had one before. He also brought toys and baseball equipment for the kids.

During the 2023 season, Rodríguez became the second Mariners player after Alex Rodriguez to achieve a 30–30 season with at least 30 home runs and 30 stolen bases. Julio Rodríguez hit 32 home runs and stole 37 bases that year.

Rodríguez (*right*) celebrates with Corey Seager of the Texas Rangers after the American League's 3–2 win at the All-Star Game in 2022.

Rodríguez hits a two-run home run during the 10th inning in a game against the Los Angeles Angels in September 2023.

Rodríguez hit his 30th home run of the 2023 season during a key game with the Los Angeles Angels. Rodríguez's homer tied the game in extra innings. But the Angels pulled out an 8–5 victory and knocked the Mariners from the playoffs. Rodríguez was happy with his great season, but team success was more important to him.

Despite a winning 2023 season with 88 wins and 74 losses, the Mariners missed the playoffs by one game. They finished third in the AL West. That season, Rodríguez was one of the best players in the league at batting, baserunning, and defense. He got a large bonus for playing so well. He used some of the money to buy his mom a new Jeep for Christmas.

In 2024, Rodríguez's third MLB season began slowly. Injuries slowed him down throughout the year. But based on his skill and talent, Rodríguez will be one of MLB's brightest stars for many years. Mariners fans can't wait to see the young all-star smash more balls and break more records.

SUPER SPORTS SCOOP

Rodríguez was the 44th player in MLB history to achieve a 30–30 season. He also wears number 44 for the Mariners. Only 46 MLB players are in the 30–30 club.

JULIO RODRÍGUEZ CAREER STATS

GAMES PLAYED: **335**	BATTING AVERAGE: **.278**
HITS: **377**	HOME RUNS: **62**
RUNS SCORED: **205**	RBIS: **192**

Stats are accurate through May 20, 2024.

GLOSSARY

All-Star Game: a game played in the middle of each MLB season honoring that season's best players

amateur: an athlete who plays a sport without being paid

contract: a written agreement, often between an athlete and a team

debut: a first appearance

minor league: a pro baseball league below MLB

playoffs: a series of games played to decide a champion

prospect: a player who is likely to succeed at a higher level of play

RBI: short for *run batted in*, a run that is driven in by a batter

rookie: a first-year player

roster: a list of players on a team

strike zone: the area over home plate through which a pitched baseball must pass to be called a strike

umpire: a baseball official who rules on plays

SOURCE NOTES

6 Victoria Hernandez, "Seattle Mariners' Julio Rodríguez Extends Historic Hot Streak after Breaking a 1925 Record," *USA Today,* August 20, 2023, https://www.usatoday.com/story/sports/mlb/mariners/2023/08/20/seattle-julio-rodriguez-extends-record-breaking-hot-streak/70636806007/.

10 Maria Torres and Corey Brock, "How Mariners Rookie Julio Rodríguez Became the New 'King of Seattle,' " Athletic, October 4, 2022, https://theathletic.com/3652799/2022/10/04/julio-rodriguez-mariners-rookie/?access_token=12803929.

19 Larry Stone, "Prospect Julio Rodríguez's Talent, Charisma Can Make a Believer out of Even Cynical Mariners Fans," *Yakima (WA) Herald-Republic,* October 16, 2019, https://www.yakimaherald.com/sports/professional_sports/mariners/larry-stone-column-prospect-julio-rodriguez-s-talent-charisma-can/article_7193c227-2f47-504c-87bd-e20a29b5454d.html.

20–21 Jesse Sanchez, "Meet J-Rod, MLB's Next Superstar," MLB.com, September 2, 2021, https://www.mlb.com/mariners/news/featured/julio-rodriguez-mlb-s-next-superstar.

23 Corey Brock, "Mariners' Julio Rodríguez Makes First MLB Homer Count: 'It Couldn't Have Come at a Better Time,' " Athletic, May 2, 2022, https://www.nytimes.com/athletic/3288123/2022/05/02/mariners-julio-rodriguez-first-home-run/.

LEARN MORE

Anderson, Josh. *Seattle Mariners.* Parker, CO: Child's World, 2024.

Baseball Facts for Kids
https://kids.kiddle.co/baseball

Fishman, Jon M. *Baseball's G.O.A.T.: Babe Ruth, Mike Trout, and More.* Minneapolis: Lerner Publications, 2020.

Julio Rodríguez Facts for Kids
https://kids.kiddle.co/Julio_Rodríguez

Leed, Percy. *Pro Baseball by the Numbers.* Minneapolis: Lerner Publications, 2025.

Seattle Mariners Official Site
https://www.mlb.com/mariners

INDEX

PHOTO ACKNOWLEDGMENTS

Image credits:, AP Photo/Aaron Gash, p. 4; Bob Levey/Getty Images, p. 6; Logan Riely/MLB Photos/Getty Images, p. 7; Greg Balfour Evans/Alamy, p. 8; AP Photo/Tracy Proffitt/Four Seam Images, pp. 9, 16; AP Photo/Sue Ogrocki, p. 11; chriss73/Alamy, p. 12; AP Photo/John Froschauer, p. 13; Jamie Schwaberow/Getty Images, p. 15; AP Photo/Zachary Lucy/Four Seam Images, pp. 17, 18, 19; Koji Watanabe/Getty Images, p. 21; Steph Chambers/Getty Images, pp. 22, 26; Denis Poroy/Getty Images, p. 23; AP Photo/Abbie Parr, p. 25.

Cover: AP Photo/Lindsey Wasson.